PRAISE FOR LIVING BEYOND THE WAVES

"I read Living Beyond the Waves and entered into the realm of dreams. How can you not? Jamieson's words carry us into an easy, deeper light of love. With empathic knowing of our mutual journey here. Captured in phrases of wisdom. Therein is the comfort of such a collection of grace such as this."

Lori Jane Day

"Jamieson allows you to see the cracks in the pavement of life, acknowledge that bad things happen to good people. He doesn't stop there, though, helps you to see that without experiencing bottom you won't reach for the stars. A real positive voice in the poetry genre; uplifting and supportive. Dreams really do come true, and the proof is positive in this delightful tome of verse. 'Living Beyond the Waves' is a must have for anyone who 'feels' life."

Sylvia Naomi DeBruyn

PRAISE FOR TALKING TO THE SKY, WALKING ON THE EARTH
and DANCING WITH THE FLAME

"As the title implies, the author Jamieson Wolf uses the words to move through what could be dangerous topics to other, less-assured writers. With almost musical tempos in some poems, more staid and cautious tempos in others, Wolf brings words to life the way master poets do. He makes the reader slow the crazed pace of life and soak up a positive story of strength. I was reminded time and again throughout the poems that a person's strength comes from within...but each one of us is allowed to see and accept the

1

help of strength in and from others. It's a lovely, empowering message to find and absorb, and I'm pleased to recommend others grab up this collection of poems to find that message for themselves."

Sandy Lender, Author of Choices Meant for Gods, Choices Meant for Kings and Choices Meant for All

"Expect the unexpected and be pleasantly surprised. Keep an open mind and heart and travel along with this author on a journey through life. Experience with him just what he has been living with and through this last year. I challenge you to change your thinking and attitude with this book. Bring on the adventure as you travel with him and get Talking to the Sky yourself."

Elaine Breault

"I have had the pleasure of reading this collection a few times and will many more I am sure. Jamieson's words provoke the entire spectrum of emotions in his words, allowing feelings to surface in the reader easily. There is an almost haunting permanence in the stories he weaves, one that has taken me to my own experiences that I thought were long lost. This poet is magical. His words are powerful and loving. A very very good read!!"

Dava Gamble, Author of Silver Journey's Silver Beginnings and Silver Cusp

"With his unique style and powerful imagery, Jamieson Wolf lures us into this beautiful volume of poetry. Colors splash across the page, emotions are captured in a single word or phrase. We ride the city bus and see a woman's tears, feel the touch of a caring hand, experience the joy in a child's smile.

We walk a city street, hushed with snow. Friends and lovers meet with a warm breath on the cheek, a kiss, a sad goodbye. We witness courage, personal growth, moments of humor, strength, snatches of a dream.

Each poem is a stolen moment in time, raw, vivid, and intimate. Touching the Sky is an uplifting affirmation of life not soon forgotten."

Dianne Harstock, Author of Alex, Without Aiden and Philips Watcher

Living Beyond the Waves

~ poems ~

Jamieson Wolf

Living Beyond the Waves

Copyright© 2017 Jamieson Wolf

 ISBN: 978-1-928101-09-3

Cover Artist: Jamieson Wolf

Text: Jamieson Wolf

Wolf Flow Press

www.wolfflowpress.com

For my Wonder Mom and my Wonder Mom in Law

A Note About Living Beyond the Waves

Talking to the Sky was about finding my voice again. _Walking On the Earth_ was about coming to terms with my life as it is now and the healing power of love. _Dancing with the Flame_ was about loving all of myself and learning to dance with life. So, what's the overall theme of _Living Beyond the Waves_?

Often, I find that I fall into what is safe, what is comfortable. I am a creature of routine. In 2016, I pushed beyond the pull of the water and really engaged with life, really tried to live as hard as I could and embrace what I found terrifying. I wanted to live beyond the comforting waves of safety and experience what was unknown.

There are a multitude of people who helped me along the way with this collection: Wonder Mom and Wonder Dad, thank you for your guidance and your strength. Kimberlee, my Writing Sister, thank you for being a light in my life. Meaghan, thank you for bringing joy to my life and for being so wonderful. Karine, thank you for being so awesome. Alexandra, thank you for your friendship and your love. Rachael and Stephanie, thank you for giving me sanity when I need it. Sandy, thank you for your wisdom and your guidance. Helen and Bev, thank you for being part of my family and letting me be part of yours.

Most of all, thank you to Michael. Thank you for loving me and letting me love you in return. You've shown me that true love does exist outside of fantasy and storybooks and I am so thankful for you as we begin the next chapter of our lives together.

Jamieson

Living Beyond the Waves

~ poems ~

Jamieson Wolf

Keeper of Wishes

They would find me at night:
small balls of light
that shone and pulsed
in tune to the words
that were being uttered
from within the orbs:
"I wish I was more popular."
<u>"I wish I was more beautiful."</u>
"I wish that he loved me."
I would touch one of the
balls of light and would be shown
the person's face. I would know
instinctively how to find them,
what their names were,
everything about them.
I would clasp their orb of light
close to me as I went
in search of them,
keeping it safe as I travelled.
With their wish, they had given away
their light and I knew that
they needed it back.
I could answer their wishes in a way,
I could help them be happier
with who they were.
By sending their wish out to
the cosmos, they had

13

sent out a piece of themselves
with it by filling the wish
with so much need and so much
intent. They did not know it
but they had sent out parts
of their soul, had diminished
their light, even if it was just
by the smallest degree. They needed
it back. I wondered what to do
while I kept their wishes safe,
pondered on it, thought of the
power of wishes, an ordinary magic
that everyone can do. However,
all magic has a price, even if it's
something as simple as a wish.
As I contemplated, my own light
began to grow stronger,
the light increasing with each
moment of intense thought.
Then it occurred to me what I
could do for these people that
needed their light back. I sat
with each wish and added a bit
of my own light to the orb,
filling each with a message.
"You are loved by the people that matter."
"You are beautiful outside as well as in."
"Love yourself first and love will follow."
I sent each of the orbs sailing

out of the window. Soon, the sky
near my apartment was filled with
hundreds of glowing orbs,
each pulsing and glowing with its own
bright and brilliant light, so bright
that it was as if the sun had chosen to glow
within the dark. As the wishes went back
to the people that had made them,
I watched them and, taking a deep breath,
made my own wish, in hopes that someone
would hear it.

__The Love Tree__

I was wandering
in the forest.
The sky was
filled with stars
that shone bright
lighting my path
and leading the
way, shining yellow
against an indigo
sky. I could see
red ladybugs flying
past me and
landing on leaves
as green as
an emerald. I
walked further and
watched as the
sky turned to
daylight, the orange
sun brilliant against
the blue sky.
I came upon
a tree covered
in violet coloured
flowers. There were
words written on
the leaves and

I tried to
read them, but
time passed quickly
here. The leaves
turned brown and
were swept off
of the tree
by the wind,
words floating into
the distance to
make a poem
in the sky.
Only one leaf
was left upon
the tree. I
wondered what word
was written upon
it and got
closer so I
could see. The
leaf was still
bright green and
I leaned in
close to read
the scrawl of
letters upon its
surface. It read:
LOVE.
As I wondered

about what love
was to me,
I heard a voice
on the other
side of the
tree. Looking through
its branches, I
saw you there,
calling to me.
I touched the
tree branches to
get a closer
look at you
and the tree
erupted into bloom,
leaves of every
colour imaginable covered
its surface. The
light around you
grew brighter still.
I walked around
the tree, stepping
over a small
stream, the earth
under my feet
lush and green,
the air around
me smelling of
honeysuckle, the fire

of the sun
bright against my
skin. I went
to you and
embraced you. As
I felt your
heart beating in
time with mine,
I let out
a breath I
hadn't even known
I was holding.
The rainbow coloured
leaves flew from
the tree, filling
the sky like
shimmering lights and
I was content
in the knowledge
that I finally
knew what love
really was.

The Uninvited Guest

The air around
us was hazy,
as if I were
seeing it through
a gossamer film.
They sat across
from me with
looks of concern
etched on their
faces. The blonde
one said simply:
"How are things going for you?"
I tried to
convey my frustration.
**"Well, he won't leave. I don't know what else to do. He just
showed up one day and won't leave. I don't know how to make
him."**
The brunette gave
me a kind
smile. She touched
my knee softly.
"Well have you tried talking to him?"
I nodded vigorously.
**"I've been nice about it, telling him that it's not just working
out, nothing against him or anything. But he won't listen."**
The blonde one
put a finger

to her chin.

"Weren't you telling us last week about his cousin? Angus or something?"

"Angry Angus. Yeah, he came to stay for a bit, but him I did get rid of. But the other one won't go, this Max Shadow person. He won't leave. I've tried everything and he won't go."

"Maybe he isn't supposed to."

The brunette said.

"What do you mean?"

"Well…"

Here she looked
at me with
a knowing glance.

"Sometimes, people or events come along for a reason. We just have to find out what that reason is."

I considered her
words. I tried
to think of
the reason why
Max Shadow was
there. I shrugged.

"Besides, you don't have much choice, do you?"

The blonde said.

"He lives inside of you after all."

She pointed to
the brunette
with a well
manicured hand.

"She has Diana Diabetes inside of her, always trying to make her foods she knows that are bad for her."
The blonde indicated
herself laying a
hand on her heart.
"I have Cathy Cancer who is always with me, though she's currently visiting her aunt."
The blonde touched
my knee again.
"We all have uninvited guests within us. We just have to find a way to exist with them instead of against them."
The haze that
surrounded both of
them began to
grow until it
was difficult to
see. Their
features were even
more blurred when
light began to
shine through them.
"Trust in yourself."
The blonde said.
"It will become clear in time."
The light pouring
into them filled
my eyes and
I woke to
find a new

22

warmth in myself
and a wetness
on my cheeks.

You Were Loved

*In memory of Chris Seguin

I had never met you,
but as I stood in a room
filled with your family,
I came to know you.
They talked of your kindness,
your generosity of spirit,
of your intense energy
and your *joie de vivre*.
They talked of your selflessness,
your sense of humor
and your big heart
that had touched so many.
I came to know you
through the stories
of others, through their sadness
at your passing, through
their laughter at something
that you had done in the past.
During the last moments
of your life, you thought that
there was nothing, there
was no one, there was only
blackness and despair.
Seeing everyone pay tribute
to you, remember you,

talk about you, I hope you
felt the lightness seep into
the darkness and sweep it away.
I hope that, at last, you felt that light
wherever you were, that you
were looking down on us
surrounded by light and brightness.
Approaching the casket, I could
think of nothing else to say except:
"You were loved. Wherever you are now, know that you were loved."

You've Re-Written My Life

As a writer,
I look at my life
as an ongoing story,
every life-changing event
as the start of a new chapter,
words spilling across
the paper of my skin.
Until I met you,
my life had become
something of a horror novel,
my body not my own,
my steps unsure,
my thoughts grim and filled
with shadows and all manner
of darkness waiting for me,
both inside and out.
Though I was loved by many,
I felt alone in the world,
carrying only half of a heart
within me, the pages
of the book of me
filled with illegible scribbles
and ink splotches where my pen
was unable to write the words
I wanted to say.
Then I met you.
Slowly, the pages within

started to fill with something
other than darkness,
something other than shadows.
The pages became filled with
stories again rather than
splotches of ink and scribbles.
Your love for me has brought
brightness to my life and
now all the pages I write
glow with a light that is
pure and beautiful.
No longer is the story I tell
one of wanting, of needing.
Now it is a story of two hearts
that found each other
despite all odds and
the life we are building together.
You've re-written my life
and I won't skip ahead
to see what's coming.
I want to experience every moment
with you by my side
and watch as the pages
continue to glow.

Kindness Is Free

I took a
seat beside her.
The coffee shop
was bustling with
people and the
only empty seat
was beside this
woman. She had
black hair that
framed her face
like a curtain
made of silk
and for a
moment, it looked
as if her
hair was blowing
in the wind.
She was smartly
dressed as if
she had come
right from work.
She looked sad,
removed from the
world around her,
as if there
was an invisible

barrier that she
held between herself
and all of us.
I took my
tea to the
table and sat,
opening my book.
It was at
that moment she
began to cry.
Heaving sobs erupted
out of her
and I watched
as tears started
to pour from
her eyes, leaving
crystal paths in
their wake on
her skin. Others
in the restaurant
sneered at her,
looking at her
with disdain, as
if it was
unacceptable that she
would show her
pain in public.
I did the
only thing I

could think of.
I held out
a packet of
tissues to her.
"Ma'am? Here you go."
I said softly.
She looked at
me with large
frightened eyes as
if surprised I
was there. She
shook her head.
"I'm okay! I'm okay, I'm okay, I'm okay!"
I don't know
if she was
trying to convince
herself of this
or me, but
I held out
the packet of
tissues to her again.
"It's all right, Ma'am. Take them."
She did with
shaking hands and
blew her nose,
dried her eyes.
She sat there
for a moment
longer and then

got up to
go. Before she
left, she looked
right at me
and her eyes
seemed a little brighter.
"Thank you."
She whispered. I
watched her go,
hoping that with
my small gesture,
I brought her
some measure of
comfort.

Love Becomes

The first time you told me
"I love you."
something within me came to life.
It was as if a light that had gone out
flickered into being once more.
When I told you
"I love you too."
the light grew brighter,
filling every fibre of me,
so that the light could only
shine forth for all to see.
People began to remark on
how happy I was, how much
I shone. I knew it was all
because of your love for me
and the love for you
that I carried inside.
As our love has continued to grow,
it's changed the world within me
and the world around me.
The entire world was brighter,
my spirit was lighter.
You have shown me that
love is not something you do,
it is something you become.
My world has become something

altogether more wonderful
because of the love that we have
for each other, and I can't wait
to see what else the world around us
will become because of our
love.

<u>Shine Forth</u>

Your sun is
hiding behind a
cloud. I can
see it there,
a muted luminescence,
begging to shine
forth. You bring
joy to others,
even though your
sun is behind
the clouds. Know
that you are
valued and that
you are loved
and that the
world misses your
glow. Remember that
this too shall
pass, that tomorrow
is another day
and that good
things happen; you
just have to
bide your time.
I will wait
for your luminescence

to shine forth
once more, banishing
the clouds, so
that everyone can
see how beautiful
you truly are.

The Gateway

I was inside of
a house. There was
no way to know
how many floors there
were; from the outside
it seemed to stretch
right into the clouds.
From the inside, it
seemed just as big,
just as tower-like.
I stood at the bottom
of the staircase and
you were beside me.
"It's okay, you can do this."
I looked at the
stairs with some trepidation.
**"I don't know that I can. You know I can't do stairs very
well."**
You smiled at me
and took my hand,
just for a moment.
"It's okay, I'll be right behind you."
I nodded, knowing that
there was no other
choice. I started up the
steps, holding onto the
railing. I wondered at

what the woman outside
the house had said.
"If you enter and are brave enough, you will discover a gateway at
the top."
I looked at her, with
skin that seemed translucent,
as if the light would
pass right through her
if it caught her in
a certain way. I
moved closer to her.
"A gateway to what?"
She shrugged, a small
smile on her lips.
"You'll have to find out yourself."
And now we were
here, inside the house,
going up the steps
to an unknown miracle.
"What kind of gateway do you think it is?"
I asked you. I
heard your voice speaking
behind me and the
sound of it helped
calm me. When you
spoke, it was as if
you spoke to the
centre of my being.
"Who knows? There's only one way to find out."

We continued to go
higher. Every time I
stumbled, you caught me.
Every time I tripped
on a stair, you steadied me.
Every time I didn't
think I would make it,
you kept me going.
Every time I felt
like giving up,
you encouraged me and
told me that I
could do anything.
We neared the top of
the staircase and I
could feel the wind
on my face. I turned
and looked at you.
"How high have we come?"
You took my hand and
helped me up onto
the very last step.
"Let's take a look, shall we?"
There was only light
when we stepped forward
and out onto a balcony.
It looked over everything
and I saw that we
had just done what I

thought was impossible.
The house was built into the
face of a mountain and we
had just scaled its heights.
We stood there, looking
out at the land below us.
You put your arm around me
and we took in the
brightness and warmth of
the sun. Something had
changed within me. We
had done what I thought
to be impossible. We
accomplished it by looking
at it in a different way.
"You can do anything you set your mind to."
You said to me.
I could only turn
to you and put
my lips to yours,
hoping that the kiss
would speak what my
words had thus far
failed to express.
As I kissed you,
I thought of the woman's
words again:
"If you enter and are brave enough, you will discover a gateway at
the top."

I could feel my heart
opening further, filling me
with light. What locks
there were inside me
fell away at your
touch, opening the gate
wide so that only
light could shine through.
When your own gate
opened, the two hearts
beating as one, shone
brighter than the sun.

Climbing Downward

* For Rachael, with thanks and gratitude.

When the siren sounded,
we ran to the cliffs.
I would have to
scale the rock face
to find safety.
I didn't think I
would be able to find
my way to safety.
Looking downward, it seemed
to be an infinity of space
between where I was
and where I would be safe.
"Want some help?"
I turned and saw a
mystic woman. She was
dressed in a flowing garment
of silver and black;
it flowed around her in the breeze
that flowed so strongly
on the top of the mountain.
"I don't know if I can do it."
I said to her. I was so afraid,
terrified, really, when each step
could mean disaster.
She smiled at me,

and she spoke kind words
that lit a fire inside of me:
"You can do whatever you set your mind to. Come on, I'll help
you."
Slowly, so very slowly,
I made my way down the mountain
with her assistance. She watched
my every step to be sure that
it was true and stable.
She helped me to find
the footholds in the rock face,
the depressions in the rock
that I could hold onto.
She kept checking on me
to make sure that I was
all right and kept up a
constant chatter to take my
mind off of the task
we currently found ourselves in.
I just told myself to take it
one step at a time,
and tried not to think about
tumbling down the mountain,
landing in the water.
I focused on taking
one small step after another,
and part way down, I knew
that I could to this.
We passed through a veil

of mist as we finished our journey,
and it blinded me temporarily.
When we got to the bottom,
I looked back at
how far we had come,
how high we had been.
I saw flights of stairs
rising up sixteen flights.
People were still climbing
downward, milling around us.
What had seemed like a mountain
at first was now revealed
to be merely one more
obstacle that I've conquered.
One more mountain that
I've climbed down from.
I looked at the mystic
that had climbed downward
with me and could only
give her my thanks.

Tunnel of Light and Shadow

There is a twin inside of me,
one that rarely sees the light
of day, or feels the light inside
of me. He doesn't stop to ask,
to comprehend, to contemplate.
All he knows is emotion, pure
and unadulterated. However,
whereas I try to live my life
holding light,
within the light,
he knows only darkness.
As he is my twin, the yin to
the yang to my light self,
his emotions are mine.
When he takes over,
I can see myself through his eyes.
I can contemplate his actions,
try and stop him, try to hold him
back from doing something he
will regret. But there must be
darkness to appreciate the light
just as there must be light
to appreciate the darkness.
I've struggled with him,
with who he is and have
a terrible time convincing myself
that he is myself at my

darkest moments. After the whirlwind
of his emotions, I spend a day or two
taking myself to task for giving in,
for entertaining such thoughts and actions.
I get mad at myself for letting him take over
and then I get angry with myself for being angry.
It is an almost unending cycle
of self abuse and self loathing. However,
there is light at the end of the tunnel.
It shines bright amongst the shadows
that linger within me. Within that light
is my salvation, my relief, my breath.
I often see myself walking down
a tunnel, one hand holding shadows
and one hand holding light.
He's walking beside me.
Eventually, he sees how tired I am,
how weary, and he reaches out to take
the shadow. But there's light at the edges,
twinkling like stars. Just as there is
darkness within my light, adding depth
to the brightness that shines forth.
I walk to the exit of the tunnel,
the light glorious on my skin.
As I walk into the light, I look back
only once. He is standing there,
watching me go and I wonder,
fleetingly, when I will see him again.

Heart Song

I checked the mail
when I got home.
I opened the mail box
and was nearly blinded
by the light coming
from within. I shielded
my eyes and reached inside.
There was one envelope.
Looking at it, I tried to
blink past the light
to see who it was from.
When I saw the return address,
I knew it could be
only one thing. I went
upstairs, holding the envelope
so gently. While I rode
up in the elevator,
I listened to a soft
music coming from the envelope,
the light pulsing in rhythm.
I waited until I was
inside the apartment,
until I was with him,
to open it. When I opened
the envelope, more light
spilled out and I marvelled
at the fact that a simple

piece of paper could shine so brightly.
"Well, go on."
He said.
"See what it is."
I slid the paper out
and saw it for what it was.
The chains that had been
around my wrists and ankles
for so long, jingling like
Marley's ghost, fell away.
The light spilled into me
and I almost turned away from it.
It felt wrong, somehow,
that I should be feeling such joy
at what is normally a
sad occurrence. I ran a finger
over the surface of the paper
and I could swear that I could
hear it sigh in contentment.
I mentioned my thoughts
to him and he put the paper aside
and took my hands in his.
"Look at everything you've been through. You would be a different person if you hadn't been through it."
I thought of his words and
they struck a chord in me;
it rang out loud to sound out
with the small song coming
from the paper. I thought

47

of what he said. Had I
not known heartache,
I would not have looked
for something more.
Had I not known despair,
I would not have looked
for true happiness.
Had I not known solitude
when I was supposed
to be overjoyed,
I would have never
learned to be comfortable
with myself; I would
never have looked within
myself to see what I truly
wanted and what I was worth.
Had the one I had been with
loved me completely,
I would never have been found
by the one that loves me now,
each day with him a gift.
So I looked down at the paper
that to some symbolized
pain, rejection and failure,
and realized that the one
that I had been with had
given me another gift of sorts.
Through his actions, he had
forced me to forge out

on my own and to see what
I was truly capable of.
What I was truly worth.
I put my hand to the page
and said the only thing I could.
"Thank you."
At that, the light from the page
increased until it was near blinding
once more and the song coming
from the paper and from inside
of me rose to a higher pitch,
so that the home I now shared
with him, the man that
holds my heart as I hold his,
was filled with my heart song,
bright and pure and true.

The Door to Life

For some time,
everywhere I went
there was a
door that followed
me. It was
scarred and its
paint was peeling,
its door knob
was rusted. On
the door was
written one word:
Life
I would see
the door out
of the corner
of my eye
no matter where
I went. It
would appear in
front of me
while I was
walking, always a
step ahead of
me. For a
while, I was
the only one
who could see

it. The door changed
as the years
went by. The
paint changed colour,
it looked even
more aged as
I got older.
Finally, one of
my friends noticed
the door. She
nudged me in
the ribs softly.
"You know there's a door there, right?"
I looked at
her, surprised that
she could see it.
"You can see it too?"
I asked. She
nodded and said
"Of course I can. How long has that been following you around?"
I shrugged.
"Quite some time. Years actually."
She gaped at
me and said:
"Why haven't you gone through it yet?"
"Because I have no idea where it will lead."
*"Isn't that part of the fun? Life is meant to be experienced. Open
the door and find out where it goes."*
I walked home,

the door following
me. It had
begun to pulse
and shift, almost
as if it were
starting to fade.
It stood in
the middle of
my living room.
The word on
the door,
Life
had begun to
glow, the door
handle shining brilliantly.
I took a
deep breath and
reached for the
door handle, expecting
it to be
white hot in
my hand. Instead,
it was as
if a calming
breeze filled my
skin. I opened
the door slowly
and, at first,
saw only light.

Then a shape
began to become
clear. I was
looking at the
shape of a
man. He held
out his hand
to me and
I took it.
"Come with me."
You said.
"There is so much of life waiting to be explored."
I stepped through
the door and
felt my life
begin anew.

<u>Living the Dream</u>

When we talked about
living together, I never
really thought it would
happen. It had always
been my dream to
build a home with a man
who loved me completely,
to start building a life
with a man who understood
me and loved all the parts
of me, even those I didn't
love. As the discussion became
more serious and we started
looking at different places,
a tiny spark of bright, pure light
began to grow inside of me.
As we packed our belongings
to move them into our new place,
that light grew to the size of a star;
I was carrying around the
impossible, a dream that was
coming true. When all of the
boxes and tubs, the odds and ends
of our lives, were mingled
together, waiting to be unpacked,
I should have felt nervous or
afraid or terrified. Instead,

I walked around the apartment
marvelling at the chaos that
surrounded us that we would
transform into a home, the star
inside of me grew brighter and bigger,
filling me almost to the brim.
That first night, I slept so well
beside you. When I woke and
realized that it wasn't a dream,
that we had each other and
that this was our home together,
the star inside me overflowed,
my body unable to contain
the light that now spilled forth.
You were that dream made real,
that fantasy, come to life.
Living with you,
being loved by you,
has changed my life.
Every day with you is a blessing,
a wish come true. You've proven
that, sometimes, the impossible can
become possible and that sometimes,
if we're lucky enough,
dreams do come true.

Glitter and Stardust

There is a light inside of me,
made from the stars and the sun.
It shines bright and beautiful
and touches everything I do.
Sometimes, my body can't
contain the light. It flows
from my body, leaving
sparkles in my wake
as I walk. The glitter
rides on the wind until
everyone else is entranced
and they, too, are dancing.

Of Stars and Light

* *This is for Rachael who is lovely and fabulous.*

There is a joy that
comes from you and
fills others with brightness.
There is a wisdom that
resides inside of you
that is beyond your years.
Countless times, you've
given counsel and comfort,
asking nothing in return.
Your laughter is like
sweetest music; it fills
the air around it with
light. Sometimes, I
swear that I can see
stars sparkling around you
when you laugh. It is
infectious and beautiful,
just as you are. Often,
I am in awe of your courage,
your strength, your determination.
You are a joy and inspiration
to all who know you.
You are made from
stars and light and
everything wonderful.

The Tree We've Grown Together

* This poem is for Michael. Thank you for the life I have with you.

When we first started
on our journey together,
we made a seed of light.
We planted it in the ground
and over time, we made sure
that it had all it would need
so that it could grow into
something wonderful.
Our love was like water
to the seed, nurturing it
within the ground.
Our support for each other
was like the earth,
keeping it safe during storms.
Every time we said
"I love you."
to each other, that was
like the wind. And
every time we felt our
hearts growing bigger with
love for each other,
that was like the sun,
shining down upon it.
Now our seed has grown
into a tree that stretches

its branches out from
the earth and into the sky.
Its branches reach into the
clouds themselves and along
all of the branches, there are
mementos and ornaments
of the time we've spent together.
I can hardly wait to see
where the tree will take us
and how we will grow with it,
until it touches the heavens
and beyond.

A Different Kind of Love

I watched them
swim, the water
moving over their
bodies like quicksilver.
Colin swam up
to me. I was
sitting on the
edge of the pool.
"Why don't you come in and play?"
He asked me.
"The water feels really good."
I shook my
head, unsure of
what was holding
me back. The
sun came out
and it glanced
off of Colin's
skin, highlighting the
muscles in his chest.
"I want to."
He splashed me
with some water.
"So come in and play. You already got your feet wet. What's the
problem?"
I took a
moment to think

about all of it.

"I wrote my romance novels when I was unhappy. I wrote them when I had love, but it wasn't real."

Colin smiles and
sluices himself with
water so that
he is glistening.

"So?"

"So? Now I have love, real and true love."

He grinned mischievously
at me. He
swam even closer.

"Then what's the problem? Shouldn't having true love only enrich your stories? Don't you want to share that kind of love with others?"

I thought about
his words. I
had assumed that
writing romances when
I was with
someone who made
me happy would
be some kind
of betrayal. Instead,
it was a
reflection of that
kind of love.
I tried again.

"I wrote about broken men finding love in the most unlikely of

ways. I don't need to write that kind of character anymore."

Laughing, Colin splashed

me with more water.

*"So don't. You now have a different kind of love than you were
used to. So write that. And I don't think that any of them were
broken."*

"You don't?"

*"No. They were brave enough to accept the gift of love, even
though it terrified them. As you were brave enough to do with the
love you have now."*

He reached out

and touched the

place on my

chest where my

heart lay beneath.

"You need to celebrate that kind of love."

I tried one

more time to

make my case.

**"But I want to write something important, something that
touches people."**

Colin gave me

a stern look.

*"And doesn't every romance do that? Do they not connect right to
a person's heart, making them feel pure and true emotion? What's
more important than that?"*

He put his

hand on my

shoulder and looked

at me right
in the eyes.
I almost lost myself
in their colour,
a light hazel,
flecked with bits
of gold and
green. He leaned
in closer to
me and I
smelled spice and
a citrus scent.
"Listen to your heart. It knows what it wants to write. Right?"
Colin began to
swim closer to
where Percy was
waiting for him,
the water gliding
off of Percy's
body as he
stood to meet
his lover. Colin
looked back at
me, raising a
hand to his
eyes to block
the bright sun.
"Hey, do Percy and I get a happy ending?"
I laughed out

loud at the question.

"Doesn't every romance end with a happy ending?"

I stood and
went back inside,
itching to write
about a different
kind of love.

A Glass Full of Stars

It has finally happened.
After seven years,
I have been able to
break free. Part of me
expected to feel sad
at the loss, but it's
been seven long years.
That's time enough to grieve.
All day, there was a sense
of euphoria within me,
rising to the surface.
I compared it to an earthly miracle,
something you wish for
but won't happen until
you take matters into your
own hands. Behind me,
I could see the chains
whenever I turned around.
They were tarnished and old,
but they were broken
and lay behind me, scattered
like bread crumbs leading
to part of my past.
I knew I would never
go back there, would never
revisit that part of my life.
On the way home, a man

kept following close behind
me. I would turn and catch sight
of him out of the corner of
my eye and then he would be
gone. When I got home, I
came into my apartment
and found him standing there.
Looking at him, I realised that
I was looking at my younger self.
I had been downtrodden,
I had been cut off from everyone,
I had been alone, even though
I was supposed to have love.
Holding out my hand, I said:
**"Why have you been following me? I thought I left you
behind."**
He nodded, smiling at me.
"You did. Today, we're both free."
I watched as a light began
to build within him, filling him
with a brilliance that shone.
I was astounded to feel the
light inside of me that had
been building all day respond
to the light of my past self.
I looked at who I had been
and embraced him; he was still
a part of me. Part of who
I had become. I felt his

light enter me and felt whole.
He pulled back and looked
me right in the eyes.
"Never be ashamed of your past mistakes. Just embrace your
future."
He began to shine even
brighter and the chains that
were wound around both
of our wrists, the last of them,
glowed a brilliant blue
before breaking away.
He began to fade, but before he
did, he said to me:
"Have a drink for who you were, who you are and who you will
become, okay?"
When he was gone, I stood there,
free and whole once more.
I would be raising a glass
filled with stars
tonight.

Timeless Love

I stopped wearing a watch
soon after I met you.
I used to have a
fascination with time,
though some would
call it an obsession.
Every moment was catalogued,
counted and allotted.
I had nearly one-hundred
watches, each keeping time.
I could hear them ticking away
from inside my jewelry box.
I felt as if time was
constantly slipping away
from me, as if it were
diamond sand that slipped
through my fingers.
When I met you,
time seemed to stand still.
We've been everywhere
together, travelled and seen
parts of the world that
I had only dreamed of.
We've grown together,
each of us finally comfortable
in our own skin when we
hadn't been before.

We've loved together,
redefining for each of us
what we thought love was.
It feels as if I've known you
for all of my life but it
has only been two years.
It's been two whole years
yet it feels as if
I met you yesterday.
Though it's only been
a relatively short while
in terms of the great
expanse of time itself,
I can't picture my life
without you. You've given me
a timeless love that, until now,
has only been found in books
or movies. You've proven to me
that real love, timeless love,
does exist. I have stopped
counting the seconds, minutes,
hours and days that make up
my life. Now there is only
the brilliant light of the future
and the time that we have
together.

Share the Joy

I was getting
off of the
elevator when a
voice called out
from around the corner.
"Hello? Are you the flower man?"
I turned the
corner and spied
a little old
lady standing in
her open doorway.
She was the
neighbour I had
never seen. She
had a kerchief
on her hair
decorated with brightly
coloured flowers and
it was also
covered in sparkles.
"I must look a sight."
She said, smiling.
"He called to tell me my flowers are coming and my hair was a
mess. I'm sure I look horrible!"
She let out
a belly laugh
of a chuckle

and I smiled.

"No, you look beautiful. I love the sparkles."

She reached up

a hand to

touch the kerchief.

"Isn't it lovely? My great granddaughter gave it to me when I saw them last."

"When was that?"

"Almost three years ago now. She's grown up to be quite the lady."

"I'm sure she has."

She looked into

the hallway again

and smiled at me.

"I don't know what's keeping him. Maybe he got lost in the building."

"Did you want me to go down and see if he's in the lobby?"

I spotted a

walker behind her

and she was

holding onto the

doorframe for support.

"No need, dear, that's kind of you. I'm just excited to get the flowers!"

Her joy was

infectious and I

smiled again, feeling

so much light.

"Is there a special occasion for the flowers? Is it your

birthday?"

"No, dear, I stopped having birthdays when I turned eighty. No, the flowers are to celebrate the birth of another great grandchild! My grandchild Josie had another baby girl!"

"That's lovely, congratulations!"

"That's sweet of you dear. They said that since I couldn't be there with them, I could at least share the joy."

I thought of
the idea, sharing
joy with others,
even if they
are far away.
I thought of
this woman, my
neighbour, bursting with
so much joy
that it was
making me joyous, too.

"You tell them that that was a wonderful thing to do. What are you going to do to celebrate?"

She let out
a little laugh.

"I'm going to have a glass of wine, put on some nice music and look at my flowers."

As if on
cue, we heard
the elevator doors
and a man
carrying the largest

vase of flowers
that I had
ever seen strode
towards us. I
smiled at him.
"She's been waiting for you."
When she saw
them, I thought
she would burst
from the joy,
her face shining.
Instead, it lifted
the spirits of
both the delivery
man and myself.
He had had
a grumpy look
on his face
before, but now,
much like me,
he was smiling.
"Oh, you do know how to spoil an old lady. Bring them into my
dining room if you could and put them on the table. And dear-"
She reached out
and took my
hand, giving it
a little squeeze.
"Thank you."
The door closed

behind her, but
her joy flowed
out of her
apartment in a
wave of sparkles
and light. I
rode the wave
of joy home.

The Road of Yellow Brick

As I walked, I could see
yellow bricks being left
behind with each step.
They sparkled like real gold
in the afternoon sunshine.
I looked behind me,
watching as they formed
a path, leading back into
my past. I kept walking forward.
I held my partner's hand
in my right and my
mother's in my left.
As we walked, the sun
overhead, casting shadows
into my eyes. One of the
shadows moved closer
to me, taking on shape
and form. Soon he, too,
was walking with us.
I knew who this was,
this dark shape, this
shadow form. He was
who I had been before.
He kept up for a while,
finding balance on the
road of yellow brick.
However, I was faster

than he was, stronger
than he'd been. Though
he tried to keep up, he was lagging
and his shape was starting
to lose its clarity. As we
moved past him,
I looked back one final
time to see him waving at me,
urging me forward.
"You got this."
He said. His voice found me
upon the wind that blew
by me. The bricks were
brighter and I could still
see them in my eyes
when I turned to look
forward again. I would
always be on the road
of yellow brick, but
I would look forward to
what would come instead
of looking back at where
I had come from.
Squeezing both my partner's
hand and my mother's, I said:
"We got this."
I felt the ground tremble
and saw a sea of yellow bricks
erupting from the ground

like flowers. I would just
have to keep walking,
keep doing what had
once been impossible,
to find out where
the road of yellow brick
would lead me now.

Mom

*For my Wonder Mom

When I was
afraid, you taught
me about
courage.
When I thought
I was too
weak to go
on, you taught
me about
strength.
When I didn't
think that I
could do something,
you taught me
wisdom.
When I was
ready to give
up, to turn
towards the darkness,
you showed me
how much I
still had to
live for.
And when I
had given up

and sworn that
I would never
love again, you
taught me about
what Love really
is. For all
of this and
more, I am
thankful. You gave
me the foundations
that I needed
as a child,
gave me what
I needed to
build upon those
foundations as a
teenager and as
an adult, you
have given me
the courage, strength,
wisdom and love
to reach for
the stars. I
am thankful for
you and have
no words to
describe my thanks.
I am the
man that I

am today because
of you and
hope that I
make you proud.
I love you,
Mom.

Man in the Mirror

Three years ago,
I met the
person that lived
inside of me.
For months, he
had been plaguing
me with falls
down stairs, with
the loss of
eyesight and speech,
and a host
of other problems.
It was when
I lost the
ability to speak
that I was
made to go
to the doctors.
All throughout the
testing, he had
remained quiet. For
months, he had
remained quiet, but
I could sense
him growing stronger
within me. An
unnamable beast that

resided within my
skin. I sat
in a room
with the doctor
and he had
looked at me,
not with pity
but with apology.
I knew what
was coming would
not be easy.
The invisible beast
grew restless inside
of me. The
doctor sighed and
then he spoke:
"There's no easy way to say this. I'm afraid it's M.S."
My mother hung
her head as
if she had
been shot, but
I sat there,
numb and afraid
to move. The doctor
went on to
talk about treatments,
all the while,
the twin inside
of me was

laughing. For a
moment, I thought
my life was
over, that life
as I knew
it had stopped.
We stood and
thanked the doctor
for his help
and I went
to the washroom
to throw some
cold water on
my face. I
looked at myself
in the mirror.
I didn't look
different, but I
felt different. It
was as if
something had changed
within me. I
could hear him
laughing inside of
me. I gave
him a stern
look, knowing that
I was looking
right inside myself.

"I know your name now, Max Shadow. I know what you are."
I heard more
laughter and a
voice said quietly:
"So? What are you going to do about it?"
I let steel
run through my
spine and looked
even harder at
myself, knowing that
he could hear
my every word.
"I'm going to fight you and I'm going to win."
He laughed again.
"You sure about that?"
I gave my
reflection a little
smile and felt
him shudder slightly.
"Yes. I am."
"You don't have the guts to take me on."
My smile widened.
"Watch me."
I turned out
the lights and
left him in
the darkness.

The Path to Self

My life is marked
by a series of memories.
If I look behind me,
I can see them forming
the path that I am on.
The memories are shaped
like paving stones or
Tarot cards, each of them
a doorway or window
into that moment,
into that memory.
As I walk along my path,
I can look back and
see where I was last year,
two years ago or three.
When I stop to touch
the memory, it rises up
in front of me, as if
it is a small television
when in reality
it is my memory I am
viewing. This one is from
three years ago, when I
was at the darkest point
in my life. I was sitting
outside on a bench and
the sun was warm on

my face. Inside of me,
however, there was only
torment. I sat on the bench
with a bottle of pills and a
bottle of water beside me.
The urge to take all of
the pills was overwhelming.
It had been a long few weeks.
May had been my dark month.
After my diagnosis, I thought
I had been doing well, that I
was fine. I wasn't. What was
a disease on top of a disability?
I could handle this, I could do this.
I couldn't. Not on my own.
I had cut everyone out of
my life. I thought it was
better that way. Even though
I knew it was foolishness, I
didn't want to infect anyone
else with my sadness. I wore it
like a shroud or cloak.
The darkness was in every
word I spoke, every action
I did. I had started wearing it
like armor, now it would
be my downfall. I called
my boyfriend at the time
and told him what I wanted

to do. I was looking for some
kind of comfort, some kind of
caring. What he said was:
"So do it."
I hung up on him and grabbed
the bottle of pills, twisted
off the cap, poured the white
tablets into the palm of my hand,
as if someone else was guiding
my actions. I remember letting
out an anguished sound,
not a yell, more like something
primal with no classification.
I forced my hand to put
the pills back in the bottle,
put them down and picked
up my phone again.
I called my mom.
I told her what I wanted
to do, what urges I was
feeling. She said the words
that saved me:
"I didn't raise a quitter. Don't you quit on me."
I remember sitting outside
on that bench, the sun still
warm upon my face,
letting my sadness leak
out of me in a flood of tears.
There was a moment that

I could barely speak but
my mom spoke to me,
told me how strong I was,
how brave I was, how I
was better than this, that
I could do anything I
put my mind to.
Slowly, I calmed my breathing,
I calmed my heart.
I told my mother:
"I love you."
She told me the same.
I put the bottle of pills
back into my pocket
and told myself that
I would live, despite how much
it hurt me to do so,
that I would thrive,
despite the fact that
I didn't think that I
had that much to live for.
Back on my path of self,
I stop watching. I don't
need to see anymore,
I know what came after.
I place the memory back
into the path, in the exact same spot.
I often think of throwing
that stone into the water

that runs alongside the path,
its shallow waves a constant
music. I think of burying it
within the grass, never to be
seen again. But I don't.
This stone is a reminder
of what it was like at my lowest
point and it is a reminder
of how far I've come.
I pat the stone so that it
settles into the grass,
remembering who I was
and give it one last glance
before moving forward
into who I am.

__The Written Girl__

I stare at
a blank page
and wait for
it to speak
to me. It
remains quiet for
a moment, waiting
for me to
put my fingers
on the keys.
When I do,
the white cloud
in front of
me begins to
ripple. I watch
as words form
on the page
and those words
begin to make
a shape, that
of a young
girl. She gazes
out at me,
her skin made
from words that
I have yet
to write. Her

eyes look at

me pleadingly and

she opens her

mouth. I do

not expect to

hear her voice.

"Why haven't you written my story yet?"

She says. Her

voice is a

soft lilt, like

music or the

song of birds

in flight.

"I don't know who you are."

I tell her.

None of my

current works in

progress feature a

young girl. I

have a few

on the go

and there isn't

a girl in

any of them.

"That's because you haven't written my story yet. You have to give me a voice if I'm to live."

I shake my

head, trying to

find the words.

"You aren't real. You'll just be something I made up."
She laughs and
I hear the
sound of bells
ringing. She looks
at me sternly.
"Doesn't every writer put some of themselves into the characters
they create? Don't they say that to know a writer, you have to read
what they've written?"
I'm nodding at
my computer screen.
I don't expect
her to react,
thinking that this
is all in
my head. She
puts her hands
on her hips
and tosses her
hair. I look
closely and read
the words that
make up her
hair. I see
the words *Queen,*
magic, betrayed, lightning,
Lavender Man, familiar,
the last Witch.
I wonder if

her hair reflects
her story. Her
dark eyes look
into mine, beseechingly.
"Can you please tell my story? I've been waiting ever so long."
I nod and
then say one word:
"Soon."
She sighs with
contentment and I
watch as the
words and letters
that make up
her body begin
to drift across
the page, unwriting
her. She looks
at me again.
"Don't forget. Don't forget me, okay?"
"I won't. I promise."
I tell her.
She gives me
one final smile
and then the
final letters that
make up her
mouth and eyes
slip away across
the page until

it is blank
once more.

The Wild Word

He was reading
one of my
poems, flipping casually
through the book.

    "Do you ever write this out in linear form? Like a short story?"

I shook my
head at him.

"No. This wanted to come out as a poem."

                        "Well then it certainly has a flow to it."

"Yes, it does."

He looked down
at the book
again, somewhat confused.

    "I've never seen poetry with dialogue. Yours don't even rhyme."

"Nope. It's how they want to come out."

    "You let the poem tell you how to write? You're the writer. Aren't

                        you in control of your own words?"

I thought of
that statement. How
many times had
I sat down
in front of
my computer and
gone to write
one thing, yet
something else came
out instead? How

many times have
I plotted a
story, only to
have the characters
do what they
wanted to do
anyways? I looked
back at him.
"Well, it's kind of like this."
I said softly.
"I want you to picture it with me."

"Okay."

He said. I
picked up another
copy of my
book and opened
it. Words began
to slide out
of the book,
flowing from the
page like water.
"Inside of every writer, there is a body of water. If you can swim in it, you'll see the most amazing things…"
Water began to
rise around us,
but the water
was black like
the ink from
the page. He

watched, his eyes
full of shock.
Soon, we were
floating in it,
held by its
warm comforting embrace.
"You'll see beasts of every kind, some defying description."
Something flew overhead
and we could
see its shadow
slide along the
water. Other animals
materialized when a
bank of land
rose out of
the black water.
There were some
beasts that I
could name, others
had no name
of any kind
as they existed
only within me.
There were people
on the bank
of land and
we watched as
trees began to
grow to offer

them shade from
a glaring sun
made of words.
**"You'll meet the most amazing characters, all of them so real,
even moreso as you come to know them."**
We watched the
people wave to
us as if
welcoming us home.
"You'll witness all the ups and downs of these people."
One of the
people that was
on the bank
of land fell
as if hurt,
a few of the
others ran to
help. Blood began
to drip from
the person, it
looked like a
man, and into
the cool water,
staining it red.
Another person, a
woman this time,
went to the
one that had
fallen and pressed

her hands to
the person's chest.
We watched light
flow from one
to the other
until light and
stars changed the
blood that ran
through the water
into something beautiful.

"My job is to help them know what their story is. My job as a writer is to tell the story the way it wants to be told. It's really that simple and that complex."

When I closed
the book, the
water began to
slide back into
the ground, the
people began to
fade, letters in
the water began
to slip back
into my book.

"Every writer has access to their own well of water. If you fight the story, the well will dry up. All you have to do is have faith in yourself."

I pointed down
at the ground.
A few letters

from my book
remained there. The
letters spelled only
one simple word:
BELIEVE.
He looked at
me with new
respect in his
eyes and said:

"How much for a copy of one of your books?"

The Light of Glass

I'm walking in a landscape
filled with glass. It glitters
like diamonds on the ground,
the sparkle from it like wishes
given form. They are blinding,
but still I look. While I gaze
into the light, I see a land
that I know well, see
a terrain that I've travelled.
It moves and shifts, the ground
never staying still for long,
the sky seeming to rush down
upon it like a turbulent sea.
"Don't look too long upon that, now."
A voice says. I look up and see a man,
his hair matted and dulled with soot,
smiling at me. He motions to the
glass upon the ground that holds
the familiar path, the one I know.
"It's best not to dwell on where you've been. Only where you're
going."
I look at him and try to
detect some sort of malice but
there is only kindness coming
from him. I motion towards the glass shards,
containing the ground that will not
remain in the same place.

It is a terrain that I know well.

"How do you know what is inside the light?"

He looks at me, his green eyes flashing

like two emeralds and holds his arms wide.

"I can tell from the way you are standing. You do not look like a happy man. Looking upon the light should fill you with joy, not despair."

I walk closer to him and smell peppermint

and the scent of wild oranges.

"I've tried, I continue to try. But I trip, I fall, I get up again. I know the ground so well."

"Ah!" He says. "But you get back up again."

"Yes, so?"

He bends and picks up

a handful of the diamond sand.

"That is your own light shining through. Your will is strong. Leave this place now. It is for the lost. You belong somewhere else."

I find myself nodding in agreement,

wondering how he could see

inside of me so deeply.

"Who are you?"

He let out a laugh that sounded

like joy released, and smiled at me.

"Does it matter? Do not dwell on what has been and what was. You are not the man you were. Focus instead on your own light and moving forward."

The light from the glass

began to increase so that

it was brighter than the sun.

"It's so beautiful."

He laughed again and motioned at me.

"That is not the light from the glass. That is the light coming from inside of you."

I looked down at myself and saw

that there were several points

along my body that were

aflame with light. That light

poured out of me and shone

brighter than the sun.

I let the glass shards fall

with a tinkle and placed my hand

over the light coming form where

my heart was. It was warm and there

was a vibration coming from it

that was like its own music.

The light grew brighter still

until it was all I could see.

"Walk forward and keep walking. Shine bright and keep shining. That is all there is to it."

Then there was only whiteness and

the gorgeous hum of light

that came from within me.

The Clouds of Forever

When I came
out of the
closet, after finally
being truthful about
who I am
and what I
was, my mother's
reaction was better
than I could
have hoped for.
The only thing
she said that
worried her was:
"Now I will worry more over you. You can be hurt in a fall, in a
crash, but now you can also be hurt because of your sexuality."
I pushed that
aside, thinking she
was being silly.
Sure, I was
bullied, teased, ridiculed
but never physically
hurt. However, I
am hurting now.
I've been trying
to process what
happened, but I
can't. I've been

trying to wrap
my brain around
what took place,
but it cannot.
My spirit has
been trying to
comprehend what occurred,
but it can
only hide itself
in shock. The
whole world is
grieving and I
along with it.
These were people
that I did
not know, people
that I had
never met, but
it's as if
a piece of
me has been
lost along with
them. I feel
it inside of
me, struggling to
find light. So
I do the
only thing that
I can think

of doing. I
sit quietly, looking
at the pictures
of their faces,
at their smiles,
at the photos
from a moment
caught in time.
I say a
lament for all
of them, for
their lives cut
short, all for
being brave enough
to be their
true selves. As
I gaze at
the photos, the
light within me
grows brighter, from
a small spark
into a flame.
"I will remember you."
I say. The
flame inside of
me grows even
brighter. Soon my
skin sparkles with
it, the internal

light becoming external.

"I will remember all of you. You will live on inside of each of us and you will shine on through us."

I light a
candle and hope
that the light
can reach their
spirits, that it
can find them
amongst the clouds
of forever and
bring them solace.

The Most Beautiful

I always say
I love you.
But those words
don't encompass everything
I feel, every
emotion that runs
through my body
every time you
look at me
or run your
fingers along my
jawline. Simply saying
I love you
doesn't capture the
emotion that stimulates
my every thought
when I think
of you, so
strong that it
seeps into my
dreams. Just uttering
I love you
doesn't capture the
fact that you
are the person
I've dreamed of
for so long,

but didn't know
that it was
you that I
was dreaming of,
a dream made
real. Simply whispering
I love you
doesn't encapsulate everything
you've given me
and how you've
re-written my life
completely. So I
will simply say
you are the
most beautiful gift
that life has
ever given me
and I will
always cherish you.

The Family Tree

The idea of
family is foreign
to me. Growing
up, I had
a family, but
I always felt
like I didn't
belong. I was
the black sheep
wearing a second
skin, the unknowable
one, baring myself
to everyone,
the odd one
out. I was
alone within my
family. I never
fit in. I
wanted too much,
needed too much.
I loved the
wrong people. They
were not my
family. Since then,
I've built a
family of the

heart, friends that
I love like
sisters and brothers,
a family chosen
with the heart
and not by
chance. When I
met my partner,
I knew that
he had a
large family, a
mother and uncles,
aunts and cousins.
I worried over
this, not having
much experience at
fitting into
a family, being
part of a
tribe. I didn't have
that within my
roots, so could
I find that
within the leaves?
I approached this
family unit with
some trepidation. How
should I behave?
He looked over

at me and said:

"They're going to love you as much as I do."

Over time, I
grew to know
all of them.
They were good
people, kind people.
They proved to
me that families
didn't have to
be broken or
dysfunctional. They could
be a unit,
be a tribe.
As more time
passed, the branches
on the tree
that rested inside
of me began
to grow new
buds and grow
new growth. As
even more time
passed, I grew
to love them.
Recently, while at
a family gathering,
one of the
uncles looked at

me and said:

"I'm so glad you're part of this family."

The leaves unfurled

completely and flowers

started to bloom.

I was no

longer the black

sheep. I was

one of them.

Lost Boy Found

I was sitting in the clouds
when I first saw you.
Looking down on the world
that I'd removed myself from,
it was your light that I
saw first, that brilliant light
that shone from you, right
up to the clouds. I was
happily blinded, just for
a moment, your light being
brighter than the sun.
I looked around me and
saw a paradise that had
all of a sudden turned dull.
It was one I had created
but it was empty.
It was not paradise without
you, an empty dream
without you beside me.
I knew I had to find you,
but to do that, I would
have to set foot on
the land I had left so long
ago. I let myself fall
through the clouds,
their gossamer tendrils trying
to slow my fall to the earth.

The clouds let out a
soft whisper, as if already
longing for me. I fell to
the ground to find myself
at the entrance to a forest,
towering trees dark and
looming over me. I knew
that you were on the
other side of the forest
and that I would have
to find my way through.
I took the first step and
then another, wondering how
many steps I would have
to take until I found you.
I took another step forward
and found myself in
amongst the darkness
of shadow and twilight.
The world looked different here.
I felt even more lost, even more
confused. I knew that I
just had to keep walking
forward and that I
would find you. I could
see glints of light through
the leaves that I thought (hoped)
was your light. I moved forward.
I did not know that the journey

through the forest would last
for so long. I was still
a lost boy, no longer sure what
I was searching for. I wished
for you in the darkness,
the shadows were my blankets
against the cold. In the dark,
I wished for you. Inside the shadows,
I yearned for you, even though
I wasn't sure you existed anymore.
I spent years inside the forest,
getting to know every nook and
cranny, every brook and stream,
every bird of prey and every day,
I still wished for you.
I no longer remembered what
you looked like, I could only
picture your light and imagine
its warmth. One day, I finally
gave up hope. I let go of
the wish and watched it fly
away from me, through the leaves
of the trees that were high above me.
I walked on inside the forest,
Shadow and Darkness old friends
by now, their voices like the wind.
I missed the whisper of the clouds.
Still, I walked forward. I could see
a chink of light through the

trunks of the trees, could hear
something moving in front of
me, coming closer. Shadow and
Darkness flew away, afraid of the light.
I stood there, afraid of what
had come looking for me,
terrified of what had found me.
Then, the light grew even brighter
and you were standing in front of me,
a silhouette that shone bright.
I walked towards you.

"You found me."
I said.

"I've been wandering forever, searching for you."
You regarded me, your features
becoming clearer as my own light
started to shine. You took my hand.
"I've been searching for you."
You said.
"I wasn't sure you existed, but you are proof that dreams do come true."
We watched as the trees
began to twist and bend,
giving us a way through.
We walked forward,
no longer lost.

An Ocean of Time

When we were
younger, we spoke
our own language.
It would be
undecipherable to the
casual listener, but
it was our
own tongue, one
that only we
could understand. As
we grew older,
teachers would keep
us apart in
different classrooms, afraid
that we would
cheat on tests
by delving into
the other one's
mind to see
what he saw.
This was a
falsehood, but the
one thing that
has held true
to this day
is that we

feel each other's
pain. I could
be miles away
from him and
have no way
of knowing what
he was doing,
but yet would
know with absolute
certainty that he
was in trouble.
This was the
case this week
when my left
eye started hurting
and parts of
me simply throbbed
in agony, yet
looked completely fine.
My head ached
and walking was
more difficult than
usual but I
could find no
cause. When my
mother called, she
told me that:
"Your brother has new symptoms. His eye is swollen and he's
having further complications. It may be new developments in his

illness…"
As she talked,
I felt this
immediate sense of
relief, followed by
a hollowing out
of grief. Relief
because the symptoms
were not my
own, grief over
him, even though
he did not
want it. An
ocean of time
separated him from
me, twenty years
of silence. Yet,
even though I
no longer knew
who he was
and the life
he led, he
was still my
brother. Even though
the silence was
thick like the
mist over water,
an impenetrable fog,
I still loved

him. That night,
I lit a
candle and said
a short prayer:
"Instead of feeling my pain, feel my love for you. Instead of feeling ill, I hope you feel this."
I hugged myself
tightly, hoping that
the hug and
the light it
held would be
strong enough to
make it through
the fog and
over the ocean
of time.

Sorrow and Joy

I knew it
would be a
day of opposites.
In the morning,
saying farewell to
one life and
in the evening,
celebrating another. In
the end, however,
there was joy
and sadness at
both. The funeral
celebrated a life
long lived of
a much loved
man, one who
gave his children
love and a
life filled with
happiness. As I
stood there with
the mourners, I
noticed people reminiscing
the life of
this man and
how the people
in this room

had loved him
and had been
loved by him.
There were smiles
as people greeted
others they hadn't
seen for a
while, laughter as
they shared stories
from the past
and tears as they
finally said goodbye.
With voices raised
in song, I
could feel him
there and knew
that he was
with us all.
Later, we drove
to the birthday
party, celebrating a
life lived for
seventy years. The
family were gathered
to cherish her
life, to share
in her joy, but
also her sorrow.
There were too

many people that
weren't there with
all of us,
too many whose
lives were taken
too soon. So
while it was
a celebration, it
was also a
remembrance for those
who were not
there in the
physical sense. However,
looking around at
all the people
in the room,
I knew that
those lost to
us were there
anyway, filling the
empty chairs amongst
us. We raised
a glass to
them and as
we all clinked
glasses, the room
was filled with
light. That light
was filled with

joy and sorrow,
pain and forgiveness.
As we drank
to them, we
remembered them. In
the end, neither
event was full
of just sorrow
or just joy.
It was all
about balance. I
knew that the
day left me
changed and even
more grateful for
the life that
I have.

A Strong Reminder

She looks at
the mark upon
my left wrist.
"What's that supposed to be?"
She almost reaches
out to touch
it. I reach
out and rub
it with my
the thumb of
my right hand.
"It's the symbol for the Deathly Hallows."
She gives me
a look, wrinkling
her face at
me and looks
back down at
the tattoo. A
thought goes off
inside her head,
as if she has
a light bulb
inside there and
she smiles at me.
"Oh! It's from Harry Potter! You must be quite the fan then!"
I nod and
say to her

"Yes, I'm quite the fanboy."
I leave it
at that. She
doesn't need to
know the real
symbolism behind the
tattoo. The symbol
refers to The
Master of Death.
That one who
has the cloak,
the wand and
the resurrection stone
will be the
Master of Death.
In a way,
I conquered my
own death. I
carry those thoughts
with me, of
how when I
first got sick,
I was lost
and had no
idea what was
going to happen
to me. I was
lost within myself,
afraid of every

sound, every movement.
If I looked
around me, I
could see the
trees of the
Forbidden Forest. I
wondered what nightmares
waited within it?
It felt as
if I had
already died, already
went beyond the Veil.
As I lost
myself in the
forest, there came
a time when
I almost let
the Dementors win,
almost let them
perform their Kiss.
However, the light
within me was
stronger and despite
my fear, my
Patronus came to
life, shining out
of me in
the form of
a wolf. I

crawled back from
death, mastering the
temptations of darkness
that wanted to
hold onto me
and went towards
the light instead,
embracing the light
within. So it's
not just a
fanboy tattoo. It's
a reminder of
how strong I
am.

__Rebuilding Home__

I never really knew
what **home was until**
I met you.
Growing up, there were
temporary shelters from the shadows,
places to lay my head down,
rooms to sleep in,
but even they had ghosts
from my past that
I carried with me.
Now, with you, I have
left behind the shadows
and the dark, and we
have built a home together.
More than that,
with every piece of furniture
that we placed,
I was putting a piece
of my heart back
where it belonged.
With every piece of art
that was hung,
I was putting a window
into my soul so that
you could see into me.
With every lamp
that was lit, it only served

to make my own light grow
bright enough so that
it shone like the sun or
wishes fulfilled.
You have shown me
that home is indeed
where the heart is
and my home is
wherever you are
because you hold my heart
so completely.

Shine Your Light

This poem is for my Wonder Mom in Law, Helen. Thank you for being so wonderful.

The first time I met you,
I was nervous. I had never
had a mother-in-law.
However, I needn't have worried.
You were as kind and selfless
as your son. As I got to know
you better, I felt the warmth
that emanated from you,
saw the light within your eyes.
At one point, you said to me:
"I don't like the way I look."
When I look at you,
all I see is beauty.
Your kindness comes through
in every touch, every hug.
Your generosity of spirit
shines out from you
in every note of concern,
every gesture that you make.
Your beauty shines forth
like a light that can
be seen by all around you.
When I look at you,
all I see is beauty personified,

as if your body and soul
are alight with flame.
I have known few people
as beautiful as you are.
So to you, I say
let your light shine brightly,
shine your light for all to see.
Beauty comes from within
and you are beautiful.

The Forest Inside

The trees have returned.
I can see them out of
the corner of my eyes,
their leaves waving
like fingers trying
to beckon me closer
so that they can wrap me
in a dark embrace.
I can feel my body
answering their shrill call,
a heaviness in my chest
that is filled with nothing but shadows.
I breathe deeply, trying
to find my centre,
trying to brush past
the well inside of
me that is filled with malaise
instead of the water and ink
that brings words.
There is no reason for the
dark forest to return,
but it is always there,
underneath my skin,
waiting to burst
forth from inside me.
A woman is walking towards me.
I almost don't see her through

the thick branches.

She puts a hand on my arm and says:

"Where are you going in such a hurry?"

I look at her and decide

that she's genuine.

"I'm trying to get away. The trees are too strong."

She gives me a kind smile.

"You carry a forest inside of you, don't you?"

I nod grimly.

"You know, if you don't let the bad stuff out, it'll push itself out in the most bizarre ways."

I thank her and move on.

The trees have grown thick around me,

the rustle of the branches,

the call of the wind

and its lullaby whisper

is almost too strong.

Something is struggling

to break free of my body.

I can feel it in my throat,

and I try to keep it down,

attempt to keep the shadows

inside of me. I'm kneeling

on the ground. I hear footsteps.

I look up to see the woman

that stopped me before.

"You have to let the bad stuff out. You can't keep it inside. Go on now, let it out."

I nod, tears in my eyes,

streaming down my cheeks.

I open my mouth wide

and a piece of shadow slips out of me,

resembling nothing but sludge.

Then, as we watch,

it begins to shape itself

into the shape of a Crow.

Its eyes regard me with

curiosity, unsure of me.

Its feathers shine like

obsidian and it ruffles its feathers.

"It's beautiful."

I whisper.

"Yes," She says. *"The darkness can be beautiful. But we mustn't let it consume us."*

"So what do I do? How do I walk away from the forest?"

I realise that she is kneeling beside me,

as she is so close. There is a warmth

coming from her that fills my body.

"You have light inside of you. Use that to banish the dark. What else can the Crow be?"

I shake my head, unsure of what to say.

"You are a writer, are you not? Why not make some ink? Fill the well inside of you with ink instead of shadows."

I blink at her and then nod.

I look at the Crow,

feel the pulse of its darkness

inside of me. I blink my eyes,

thinking of a pen, of something that

can hold ink and stories inside of it.
Wishing for something
to keep the shadows at bay,
to combat the lullaby of darkness.
When I open my eyes,
the Crow is gone. In its place
is a pen of black obsidian
and a black journal
waiting to be written in.
I look up to thank the woman
but there is no one there.
I stand as if I have just won
a battle, taking hold of the pen and journal
and I feel them pulse,
full of the stories
waiting to be written.

An Orchestra of Light, Wind and Leaves

I can hear the sound of leaves
whenever you walk,
rustling along the ground.
I look down to see if
I can spot them,
trailing merrily along after you.
Every time I do,
I am shocked to find
that there are no leaves
fluttering in your wake.
It was only when
I began to hear the leaves
sliding along the ground as I walk
that I understood.
The leaves are your music,
a soft silky sound,
like paper learning to fly.
I carry your music
inside of me,
your love for me
is like a symphony of leaves
and wind, singing its song
that fills every crevice
of my body.
I can feel them swirling
inside of me,
basking in the light

we share with each other.
That light intensifies
every time we touch,
each time we kiss.
My love for you
is its own symphony,
a swirling of leaves and wind
and so much light
that it would be blinding
to the naked eye.
When the two swirls intermingle,
a brilliant thing occurs:
the wind is replaced
by a voice that is singing,
my vision is overtaken
by the light emanating
from both of us
and every touch is a note
inside that voice,
every touch a pause
before the crescendo.
Every kiss is like a flare
of wind and light,
within that song.
We carry an orchestra
of wind, light and leaves
within us that
will continue to sing
for our song

has just begun.

What Lay Forgotten

She got on
to the elevator.
When she saw
me, her smile
brightened and her
whole body shone.
"Hi!"
She said, excitedly.
"How are you? I haven't seen you in forever!"
I looked through
my memory, the
albums of memories
that are there.
I flipped through
the place I
thought she should
be, but the
page was blank,
with nothing on it
except the words
MEMORY MISSING
written in bold
red type. I
closed the album
within my head
and looked at
her, hoping that

my smile was
convincing enough. I
offered her pleasantries
and asked if
she had vacation
planned. I didn't
ask anything personal
because I could
remember nothing about
her, not her
name, not where
I knew her
from, not even
how long I
knew her. Inside
my head, I
opened the memory
book and placed
a photo of
her, so that
it would be
there next time.
When the disease
hit, it left
me with a
battle to fight
within my own
body. It also
took something from

me. My memories.
I used to
be able to
quote from movies
on queue, remember
the plot and
title of every
book I've ever
read, every place
I've been to,
songs I used
to know by
heart. Now, all
those memory books
are filled with
blank pages, blank
faces, empty places.
After the heaviness
left me, and
I took up
the fight, my
focus was on
getting better. As
I started that
battle, I started
to realise how
quiet it was
inside my head.
I took a

look inside myself
at the boxes
filled with memory
books, pictures and
pieces of paper,
memories preserved for
later reference. I
was shocked to
find an almost
empty room instead
of a warehouse
filled to the
brim. Now there
was only one
room filled with
a handful of
boxes. As I
started to go
through the boxes,
I kept seeing
MEMORY MISSING
where a memory
once resided, its
page left with
a vague outline
of whatever had
been there before,
a shadow of
what it use

to be. At
first, this worried
me and I kept
thinking that my
boxes would never
be full again.
I lamented that
which I had
forgotten. Eventually, I
realized that, in
a way, it
was a blessing,
that everything that
had been forgotten
could be filled
with a new memory,
and that everything
I had forgotten
could be new
all over again.
I realized that
new albums could
be made and
that life didn't
have to be
spent lamenting what
I had forgotten.
That the past
was the past

and all I
had to do
was focus on
the future. I
turned to the
woman in the
elevator and asked
"I'm sorry, but could you tell me your name again?"

Magic Made Real

As a child, I used to dream
of magic made real,
of distant lands where magic
held sway, where it was a
real, vibrant thing that
coloured the sky and shone
from the eyes of everyone.
As I grew older, that dream faded,
replaced by the words and actions
of others, those so rooted in
the mundane that they pulled
me down into it and the world
no longer shone brightly.
As I grew older still,
magic could be found only
inside books because they
would never hurt me
or judge me, never mock my
dreams of flying on the back
of a dragon, or riding across
hills in distant lands that
I yearned so much to visit.
Now, I am living that dream
because of you. We have travelled
to far away worlds on the wings
of large metal birds, we have seen
strange creatures that defy description.

You have helped me to believe
in time travel; we have been together
for over two years, and yet
it feels like I met you only yesterday.
We have celebrated and created memories,
each more magical than the last.
You have given me so much.
My life is brighter
because of you and the love
that you have given me.
I believe in magic and wonder
once more and know that you
are magic made real.

The Armour Inside

My life is filled
with needles and pills.
I take an injection
every day and pills
three times a day.
At first, the act of
injecting myself each day
was a hindrance, the pills
a liability. I felt they
were a sign of weakness,
an indication that
I was somehow lesser
than everyone else.
A sign of my weakness.
The very act of having
to rely on a needle
was a daily moment of fear.
As time has passed, however,
I've grown. As I've grown,
how I view myself has
changed, a little at a time,
until the needles and the pills
just became normal,
a part of my daily routine.
Instead of something to fear,
the pills and injections
have become part of

the everyday. Now, whenever I
take my pills, I imagine
them filling me up
with light and everything good,
until I'm so full of light
that it can't help but shine outwards.
Now, when I take my injection,
I imagine that each needle
is another piece of armor
being placed inside my body,
protecting me from the illness
that resides inside of me.
Each injection is another
piece of armor, another
link in the chainmail
that is keeping me whole,
from the inside out.

To Touch the Sun

He got on
the bus wearing
a smile. I
called out to him.
"Morning!"
He gave me
a vague wave
but his smile
widened. I had
heard him mumble
a few words,
a few syllables,
to himself. Sometimes,
when he did
speak, it was
stilted, as if
the words were
weighed down by
memory and he
was unable to
pull them out.
I knew that
he was mentally
disabled but I
didn't know what
plagued him. It didn't
matter. I always

saw people looking
when he mumbled,
when he shuffled
to find his
seat, when he
made noises at
the back of
his throat. People
would stare at
me when I
spoke to him,
as if apologizing
for the fact
that he was
speaking to me.
He sat in
the seat behind
me. We rode
this way for
a minute or two,
me in my
seat, he in
his, until he
said to me:
"Do you ever wonder what makes the clouds glow so brightly?"
I turned to
face him. He
was staring out
the window at

the early morning
sunrise with childlike
wonder. I shrugged.
"I don't know. I think the sun has something to do with that."
He touched the
window, drew a
finger along the
glass as if
he were able
to touch the sun.
*"The clouds always look happiest when they're orange. I like red
clouds fine, but they look happiest when they're orange and the air
outside is crisp."*
He took a
deep breath as
if he could
smell the air
outside instead of
the stale air
inside a bus.
*"Or when the clouds are yellow. They look so happy, so full of joy.
I want to be happy like that, bright like the clouds."*
He took a
deep breath as
if he would
never get his wish.
*"I remember when my mother used to take me out to play as a
child. The sky was always pink when I was with her. I don't like
purple though."*

I had been
mesmerised by his
voice. It was
the most I
had ever heard
him speak.
"Why don't you like the colour purple?"
He looked away
from the window
and right at
me. I saw
right into his
eyes, they were
a deep and
gorgeous blue, so
clear that it
seemed he could
see into me.
"The clouds were purple on the morning my mother died."
I'm shocked by
his words and
there doesn't seem
to be anything
I can say.
I try anyways.
"I'm sorry."
I mutter lamely.
*"Don't be sorry. Whenever I see pink clouds, it's my mother
saying hello."*

The silence is
broken only by
the sounds of
the bus and
other passengers. I
think he's fallen
silent when he
speaks once more.
"It's my mother saying hello."

A Journey Through the Cards

I am on a continual journey.
I often feel like I am the Fool
from within my deck of Tarot cards.
I am standing at a precipice
looking around me at the world,
not as I knew it, but as I know it now.
I've been on this journey for years now
and have met many obstacles.
There have been times when
I wanted so badly to give up,
when the Swords showed their edge
and drew blood. But Swords are two-sided,
so that at other times, they helped me
to rebuild the Tower that had fallen to the ground.
When I started to get better and believe
in my own magic, in what I could create
and the strength of my spirit,
it was the Wands who were my guides,
lighting the fire inside of me
so that it burned bright and strong for all to see.
They urged me to create, to live, to dance.
I did not have to do this journey alone.
My Cups overflowed with people
that I met along the way or that I already knew,
some who would lead me towards my Strength,
like the Empress or the Princess of Pentacles.
Yet there were those who would want me to be

156

the Hanged Man like the Devil who wanted
to keep me down. Still I ventured onward,
the ground littered with Pentacles that
shone like the Sun brought to land.
Yet it wasn't riches that I desired
but a rich life. At one point on my journey,
I looked up into the sky and saw
The Star shining so brightly.
It had been there all along, guiding me
towards my future. If I had given in,
I would not have the life I have now.
In a way, Death did come to me,
giving me an ending to something
I could no longer tolerate and
a new beginning to something new,
something wonderful. I stared up at the sky,
the seventy-eight cards fluttering
past my vision, each of them a portal
or a window so that I could look inside of myself,
see every step I had taken, the cards like
stepping stones in the darkness across the sky.
As I watched, the Star burned even brighter,
shining down upon me. I knew that my journey
was not over, but I was not alone.
I would continue, for this is my journey
and I will take it one card at a time. ·

The Daughter of Wands

* For Alexandra who fire, wind and song.

When I first met you,
I was struck by the light
that emanated from you.
As I came to know you better,
I admired your free spirit,
your willingness to love,
and your thirst to live.
You have been a constant
source of inspiration for me,
always willing to lend me
some light when the need arises
until I was able to find my own.
You are a visionary, always able
to look into the murky clouds
of the future and succeed,
even when you're not sure
of the outcome that awaits you.
You are brave, able to take on
any challenge that confronts you
when most would admit defeat.
You are passionate in everything
that you take on, all that you do,
filling all those around you
with excitement. I am often
in awe of you, of how,

like a snake sheds its skin,
you cast off the parts of yourself
that are holding you back
so that you are left only with light,
with the pure vibrancy of you.
I have seen you transform
into the many facets of yourself:
Mother, friend, lover, confidant.
You are all this and more
and I am filled with wonder
at the thought of you
and what you have yet
to become.

A Map of Stars

* *This poem is for Michael. Thank you for all that you are.*

Every action
creates several possible
reactions, the outcome
of choices that
weren't made but
still trace a
path against the
stars. Sometimes, it
is as if
I can look
back through the
darkness of my
past and see
what the stars
would have brought
for me if
I had chosen
differently. If, instead
of living the
life I live
now, I had
run instead. When
I first met
you, I was
enraptured, entranced, enthralled;

I was also
terrified. I had
never had anyone
treat me as
you did, with
kindness and compassion,
with understanding and
passion. I did
not know kindness
in my life
from men, had
not known what
it was like
to be completely
accepted and even
cherished by another
man. I wanted
to run so
far away from
you but at
the same time,
there was no
way I could
have. I decided
to face what
frightened me head
on and instead
chose to love
you completely as

you did me.
I was terrified
but my love
for you was
stronger than my
fear. I look
back across the
black sky shining
with stars like
diamonds, each star
a mark on
the map that
we have made
together. If I
had run, I
would have missed
every moment that
led up to
the moment when
you first told
me that you
loved me, the
times we have
travelled the world,
the small moments
when I've learned
what a real
relationship is like.
I would have

missed the moment
when you asked
me to be
your husband. I
know that somewhere,
within that map
of stars, there
is another version
of me who
made a different
choice, who ran
instead of staying.
To him, I say
**"Look at everything you've missed. And everything still to
come."**
To you, I say
"I love you."
Though those words
aren't ever enough.

Taking Flight

When the darkness clears,
I am flying through the sky.
Though I know I am asleep,
I am more awake inside the dream.
Underneath me I can feel muscles
moving up and down with the wind.
I can hear the flap of wings
and see the flash of purple scales,
shining like jewels in the moonlight.
There are sparks coming off of
the scales and they float through
the darkness like stars.
I feel the dragon begin its descent
and wonder where it has taken me.
It sets down on the grass softly
and I slide off of its back.
I look around me and, through the shadows,
I see the home that I lived in as a child.
Its curtains are closed and there
is no one home, but there is a light on inside,
as if the house was expecting me.
The dragon urges me forward,
pushing open the front door with its tail.
I slip inside quietly, afraid to see what
lies in wait within the darkness.
I can hear the sounds from the memories
that are encased within the walls,

the torment that these walls entombed,
hidden from the world outside.
I take a step into the house and a breeze
follows me inside, bringing purple stars
upon it. As I look at the stars,
they fall in a path leading upwards,
footsteps appearing on the wood
as if I had already walked this path before.
I slip up the stairs, careful to step
on each footstep. Each time I do,
the sound of bells rings through the air.
The footsteps lead to my old bedroom
and the door is already ajar.
I stand in front of it and place my hand
upon the wooden surface.
I see myself as a young child and wonder
where that boy went. I feel an answering
beat inside myself and know that
I carry him within me.
Inside, the room is much as I had left it
and I head to the closet to see
if my box of treasures is still there.
The box begins to vibrate and hum softly
when it feels my gaze upon it.
I approach the box with trepidation and
anxious anticipation. I open the box,
its wood was covered in dust after so long,
and look inside. Lying nestled at the bottom
of the box, on a bed of purple felt,

is a pencil. It's yellow and has a pink eraser.
My name is written upon one of its sides.
I remember this pencil. I wrote my first story
with this pencil, wielding it like a sword on the page.
I pick it up and it starts to shine when it
comes into contact with my skin.
Purple light, so reminiscent of those stars,
begins to shine out from it and I can see
words floating through the air, words that
it had written. Soon, my bedroom is filled
with the words of all the stories I wrote here,
the stories and the words were my escape,
my safety, my refuge, my salvation.
I hear the roar of the dragon outside
and run to join him, the pencil still
spilling out words and light.
Now it's letting loose words from stories
that came after, novels and sonnets,
poems and stories, poems and prose,
so many words and each one a joy.
Outside, the words begin to float up
into the air. The dragon gives another roar
and lets out a stream of purple fire.
I run to it, clutching the pencil
in my hands. The dragon lowers his head
so that I can climb aboard and then
he takes flight. We fly up into all of
the words I have written, every syllable,
every letter. They are like clouds in the sky,

like smoke upon the water.
As we fly further, away from what I used to be
and towards what will be, I see more words
shining in the distance. These are gold in colour
and I know that they are words that
I have yet to write for my story is
far from done. I urge the dragon onward
and when we enter the glowing cloud of words
it is like entering the sun. The dragon
gives one final roar and when I wake,
there is a pencil clutched in my hand,
glowing softly and pulsing with
soft light.

The Reality of Dreaming

For as long
as I've known
you, I've felt
like I was living
inside a dream.
As if everything
that I had with
you was too
good to be
true. I was
holding on to
the dream, living
within it, enjoying
every moment that
I had with
you. Part of
me thought that
it was doomed
to end as
no one could
be this happy,
this content, this
enraptured, this joyous
for very long.
Though as time
passed and the
days turned into

weeks, then into
months and now
years, I let
go of the
idea that this
dream would fade
as all dreams
do. It still
felt as if
I was living
inside of a
dream and I
knew that I
didn't want to
wake up, that
I couldn't live
my life without
you and the
light that you
bring to it.
I began to
believe that we
would spend our
lives together, that
what we had
transcended the idea
of love and
made it into
a reality. Then

the unthinkable happened.

"You know,"

You said.

"We've been talking about having a commitment ceremony. We're doing everything but getting married. So why don't we just get married?"

There must have
been a disconnect
in my brain.
All I could
hear were the
sounds of glitter
joy and stardust
as they sped
through my head.

"What?"

I couldn't get
the words out,
didn't know what
to say, words
had left me.

"Will you marry me?"

Instead of answering
you right away,
as the words
were still trying
to find their
way back into
my consciousness, I

did the only
thing I could
think of. I
kissed you. Inside
of that kiss
were the words
that I couldn't
find, the emotions
that you stirred
in me, thankfulness
for you that
illuminated me every
day, the joy
I have of
being loved by
you. When I
broke the kiss,
there were tears
in my eyes
and you said
"So is that a yes?"
I looked you
in the eyes
and said **"Yes."**
I realized then
that I wasn't
dreaming, that this
was glorious reality
and my dreams

had become real.
You have given
me a reality
that was better
than any dream.

Wish Cloud

I would have
missed you if
I had not
turned my head.
I had not
seen you in
seven years. You
had not changed
much, except for
your eyes. They
were filled with
ice when they
took me in.
Your face was
creased in anger
and I could
almost see a
large black cloud
following close behind
you. As you
neared me, there
was a lot
that I wanted
to say. Such as:
"Hello."
or
"How are you?"

or

"I hope you're well."

To think that

we had spent

five years of

our lives together,

yet there was nothing

that we could

say to each

other. You, because

the past was

still alive and

well; and me,

because I could

see that you

wouldn't listen to

anything I had

to say. The

look you gave

me as you

passed by me

would have left

me hurt and

severely scarred if

you had the

power to hurt

me anymore. I

only felt bewilderment

that you chose

to live with
so much hate.
You moved past
me and as
I watched you
walk away, I
realized that the
well that I
carried inside me
that had been
full of hurt
and pain was
now only filled
with light. I had
thought I would
be afraid of
you when I
saw you next,
but instead, there
was only calmness.
You had lost
the power to
affect or control
me. You walked
on, your shoulders
hunched against a
world that you
were determined to
be angry at.

So I did
the only thing
I could do.
I reached into
the well inside
of me, filled
with ink and
brightness and I
sent you a
little bit of
light. I watched
as the light
made its way
towards you, hoping
it would lessen
the size of
the cloud that
followed you closely.
Within that light,
I put one
wish. I said:
"I wish you well."
It was my
final gift to
you. When I
turned away from
you, I knew
that you would
remain in the past

and that I
was heading home
to my future.

Move Forward Into Story

I'm standing in front of a blank canvas.
It beckons me forward and I feel a tingling
in my fingertips as they itch for a wand
to channel creativity through.
I look down and expect to see
a brush dripping with paint
or a piece of charcoal smudging my fingers.
Instead, I see a pen gripped and ready.
It's vibrating slightly as if it already
knows what it's going to write.
I place the pen on the canvas,
as visual art is another way to
tell a story, to catch a moment in time
standing still so that we can
observe its beauty. When the pen
touches the fabric, I watch as
lines of ink flow out from the tip
of the pen. These lines swirl
across the surface and shape themselves
into a form that is taken from my memory.
The lines begin to move so the whole
picture looks as if it is real.
I see a boy sitting with a journal in hand,
clutching a pen much as I am now.
He begins scratching the paper with
his pen, making words along the page.
I watch as the worlds he's creating

come to life in front of his eyes
and the wonder he feels being able
to harness this magic. It takes me a moment
to realize that the boy is me, that this
was the moment I first put pen to paper.
I move my own pen along the canvas
and the lines move and shift once more.
As the lines begin to twist into shape,
I see a young man, holding a book he
wrote for the very first time, holding his words
as if the book were a child. The young man
turns his face and I see myself.
I look more closely at the canvas
and see the title of my first book,
the words that I had typed out
filled with their own special kind of magic.
The book itself is shining and, even through
the fabric, I can feel its pulsing heat.
I move my pen one final time,
watching as the lines shift and move
into a shape. I lean my face closer
to the canvas and see that the lines
are actually all made up of words and letters.
The lines of words shift and move
and there is the sound of bells in the air
as if something I cannot see is singing to me.
When the lines stop shifting, I am
looking at myself as I am now,
my holding a pen against a surface that is

moving and changing as I look at it.
I almost take my pen away from the fabric
when the me on the it turns and gives me
a soft smile, as if he knows my momentary fear.
I keep the pen on the canvas and watch
as the lines shift once more. They become
a doorway. The door is situated in the midst
of a meadow. I can see flowers in the grass
moving and shifting in the wind.
There is a tree in front of the door
and its branches also bend and shift,
almost as if welcoming me to enter,
beckoning me forward to the unknown.
Slowly, the doorway opens but I am
not afraid. I blink and then the doorway
is in front of me, the meadow around me.
I can hear the whisper of the wind
through the grass, hear the creak of the
tree as it continues to wave in the wind.
I hear the sound of bells again and
they sound like music. I know that
I have nothing to fear, that these
are my words that are surrounding me
and they mean me no harm. I step forward
through the door, knowing I can return
any time I want to. I may not know what
is on the other side of the door,
but the only thing I can do
is move forward into story.

The Halloween Baby

* For Bev, who brings joy.

When you were
born, the witches
gathered around you
in the darkness.
They were shrouded
by shadow and
the clothes they
wore helped them
blend like smoke
into the night.
Each of them
looked down upon
you, their eyes
shining like bright
jewels in the
twilight. The first
woman, a lady
with dark hair
and eyes so
dark it was
as if she
carried the sea
within her said:
"Give her bravery."
She waved her

hand and a
shower of silver
sparks fell like
stars upon you.
The second woman,
taller than the
first, with red
hair that fell
in ringlets down
her back and
a litheness to
her frame and
green eyes that
were bright like
precious emeralds said:
"Give her kindness."
She waved her
hand and the
air was filled
with lights that
fluttered around you
like wishes. The
third woman, a
matronly woman that
had bright blue
eyes that shone
like sapphires and
blonde hair that
fell in ringlets,

her whole form
pulsing softly with
a muted glow,
smiled down at
you and said:
"Give her a laugh that is like music that will bring joy to all who
hear it."
She waved her
hand and light
that shone like
the sun filled
your bassinet. As
the years have
passed, they have
watched you grow
into the woman
that you are
today; you are
truly a woman
of remarkable bravery,
and have overcome
that which would
have felled a
lesser person. You
are the embodiment
of kindness, always
giving from the
heart in everything
that you do.

And your laughter
is the most
musical sound that
the witches have
ever heard and
that is your
magic. It has
the power to
lift people's spirits
and banish the
darkness and shadow
that are often
after us. You
are the embodiment
of magic and
we are blessed
to know you.

Falling to Find Myself

The world was
falling
around me. I
tried to take
a step, but
the floor rose
up
to meet me,
as if it
wanted to give
me an embrace.
I knew that
something was wrong,
that my body
was not my
own anymore.
I waited months
for a diagnosis,
longing to know
the name of
the beast that
now resided within
me, while at
the same time
dreading the outcome.
What shadow lay
within me? And

more importantly, could
I accept it
once it had
a human name?
While I waited,
I fell again
and again, my
body rebelling against
what I wanted
it to do.
When I did
finally get an
answer, the symptom
was like a
voice in the
wind, there but
fleeting. There, but
like gossamer within
my grasp. As
I tried to
re-learn what my
body was and
what I house
inside my skin,
I took steps
towards getting better.
I started on
the inside, focusing
on the Spirit

and then the
Heart. Only then
would I be
strong enough to
tackle the biggest
obstacle: my body.
I found solace
in Reiki, found
guidance in Tarot
cards, found comfort
in Manifestation, in
choosing my own
path. I was
still falling, still
letting the ground
rise up to
meet me, its
concrete embrace somehow
comforting because it
was something familiar
now. However, each
time I got
up, each time
I pulled my
body upright and
brushed off the
dust left behind
from my concrete
embrace, I was

stronger. Each time
I got back
up and refused
to stay down,
I found a
little bit more
of myself. I
could see the
pieces of the
chalice that had
been within me
littering the street
like diamonds, glittering
in the half
sunlight of mid-day.
I gathered each
one as I
found them, following
their luminescence towards
the future. Each
time I took
one in my
grasp, it lay
in my hand
for a moment,
but would then
sink into my
skin. I could
feel the chalice

rebuilding itself within
me, the shards
and pieces fusing
together. As each
piece found its
mate, the light
within me grew
stronger. I wasn't
just falling. I
was falling to
find myself, the pieces
of me that
I had lost.
With each piece,
I took back
more of myself,
regained the pieces
of me that
I had thought
to be lost.
Each time I
stood up again,
I wasn't merely
regaining my footing.
More than that,
I was reclaiming
myself, I was
rising
for a new

day, for a
new dawn, for
a new me.
Every time I
got back up,
I was telling
myself that the
disease wouldn't win,
and that was
enough.

You Are Made of Stars

* This poem is for my Wonder Mom.

When I think of you,
I am reminded of stars,
Stars hold magic within them,
and that magic takes form
in light, shining down
upon us from light years away.
You have always been capable
of great magic, able to mend wounds,
heal hearts or grant wishes.
Stars are wise beyond their years,
they have been helping those
that wish for wisdom
learn secrets from the skies,
teaching those that want
to learn more about the world
that surrounds them.
Stars help guide others to safety,
having guided sailors and creatures
that live within the water
to their destination on calmer seas,
and they provide light
in the darkest of times,
helping us not to feel so alone.
Though stars are far away from us,
they remind us that

we are not alone,
that all we have to do
is look up into the sky
to be close to them,
to be reminded of their light.
You are all of this
and more, a true being
of magic and light.
As you continue to shine forth
and shine on, it is an honour
and a privilege to be graced
by your light and your love.
I can only hope to shine
as brightly as you do
so that we can fly across the sky
together.

Taking Off the Mask

"You gotta be careful when you take that mask off."
She said.
I looked at
her and the
shadows that emanated
off of her.
I knew she
was going through
a dark time,
that she felt
the loss of
her husband as
if it were yesterday.
"What do you mean?"
I asked.
She gave me
a sage look
and said:
"People wear masks all the time. You never truly know anyone.
You only know what they show you."
I thought of
what I chose
to show the
world, what I
chose to let
others see. As

I thought about
this, I reached
up to touch
my face, to
see if I
could feel any
masks there. I
didn't feel any
ridges or markings
that would denote
a mask. I
wondered if I
lived without one.
Later, while walking
on the sand,
the ocean filling
the air with
its music, I
looked at the
man I loved so
deeply. I could
see no mask
there. Even so,
I reached up
and touched his
face and felt
a ridge there.
I slowly pulled
the mask away

only to see

his face just

as I knew

it. He reached

up and pulled

away the mask

I wore, too.

"Do I look different?"

He shook his

head and said:

"You look just as you always do to me. Beautiful."

It occurred to

me that maybe

there were people

we were comfortable

enough to just

be ourselves completely,

and what a

marvelous gift we

had given each other.

I took his hand

and we walked

on, letting the

masks fall away

to the sand.

Shine Your Light

This poem is for Meaghan, who is a Star.

 There is a
light that comes
from within you.
At first, I was
blinded by it,
I would look
upon you and
see only stars.
Every time you
moved, it was
like you were
conducting the Milky
Way, a thousand
stars would trail
after your fingertips.
As I got
to know you,
the stars that
made up your
light gained a
brilliance matched only
by comets as
the shine across
the sky, the
light within you

growing beyond what
the eye could
see. I would
watch as you
helped others, filling
up their lives
with light. Each
time you did,
I could see
stars lingering on
their skin, stars
that would glow
with a soft,
comforting light. Soon,
the world around
you was filled
with people that
shone because of
you, whose lives
were brighter because
you were in
it. Then came
a time where
the stars that
came from you
darkened, the shine
was dulled and
the air around
you filled with

shadow. To help
you through this
shadowland, I held
out my hand
to you and
gave you some
of my light
so that you
would find your
way back to
yourself. At the
edge of the
barrier between light
and dark, I
say to you:
Never forget that
you are a
being of light,
a person of
such beauty, both
internal and external.
Never doubt for
an instant who
you are and
what you are
capable of. You
hold the world
in your hands.
Shine your light

and leave the
shadowland behind. The
world is more
beautiful because of
you.

The Dream Reality

Inside of the dream,
we were walking in a valley.
There was cobblestone and grass
underneath our feet, flowers lining
the path we were on. As we walked,
we began to see others waiting
alongside the road. On either side,
there was everyone we knew,
all wearing white so that they shone
brighter than the sun above us.
I held your hand and felt your light
shining within mine so brilliantly.
Those that lined the path were smiling,
radiant and joyful. I could feel the joy
inside of myself, radiating from inside of you.
As we walked further down the path,
I heard a woman's voice break out in song;
lilting and beautiful and filled with light.
We walked towards that voice that filled me
with such happiness and hope
that it made my spirit want to sing with her.
You clutched my hand tighter and I returned the gesture,
knowing that my life was about to change.
You looked at me and I could only see your light,
shining so brightly.
I wake at that moment,
slowly, and look around me expecting to see

a valley filled with our loved ones,
still hearing that lilting song that called to me.
I turn and look at you, lying beside me
and I marvel at the changes that we have
made together, at the changes within me
since I met you. You have shown me such love
that you've taught me to speak
the unknown language of the heart.
I can feel the pages of the book that this is written on
fluttering inside of me as I try to find the words
to tell you what you mean to me,
as I try to encapsulate the emotion you evoke in me
into one word or one phrase. I lean close to you
and whisper "*I love you*" and hope it will be enough.
As we prepare to take that next step in our journey,
and continue down the garden path that I saw
inside my dream, I know that making that dream
a reality is the greatest gift you could give me.
Inside myself, I hear the fluttering of pages
and the lovely lilt of song.

The Brightest Light

I am walking in the dark.
The air is so crisp that
my breath forms clouds in the sky.
They float away from my lips,
word-shaped and almost translucent.
Watching them fly above me,
I watch as light from the stars
shine within them. Words like
joy, hope, celebration. Words like
togetherness, family, kindness and *cheer.*
I watch as the words disappear
into the velvety darkness of the sky
which is broken only
by the smallest pinpricks of light.
As I make my way over the ground,
everything sounds like music:
the crunch of my feet on the snow,
the soft sound of the wind swirling
around my face, the soft tinkling of
icicles dancing in the cold winter wind.
It is as if the world itself is an orchestra,
and I am its audience. As I walk on,
I begin to notice a light
almost pulsing along the snow.
It creates shadows that move and shift
almost as if the light is trying
to chase the shadows away.

I follow the shadows to the source
of the light and watch as a brilliant star
shines in the sky. I feel a lessening
of the darkness in the world around me
as the daylight returns, oh so slowly.
I look deeper into the star above me
and within it, I see a wheel turning
at its centre. The wheel turns slowly
and I realize that the pulse of the star
and the shadows that move
across the snow follow that pulse,
that movement. It is as if the star
is the sun and the moon combined,
and the veil between the night and the day
are growing thinner and the darkness
is letting light through. I stand there
beneath the star that is also
the sun and the moon at once and
I feel its light move over me,
filling me with warmth and joy.
I am filled with hope for the light
is beginning to return. The wheel
of the year is about to take
its last rotation. There is a hum in the air
that joins the natural orchestra
that plays around me. The light begins
to grow even brighter, even more
beautiful than it was before,
shedding light in all of the shadows

around me so that all I can see is light.
Above me, the wheel that contains
the stars, the sun and the moon
shines down upon me. A small piece
detaches itself from the wheel
and falls down toward me.
I hold out my hand and the star
rests in my palm, warm to the touch
and shining with the brightest light.
Another year is at its close
and within my hand,
I hold a beginning.

The Gift of You

For Michael with love.

It seems like another lifetime
when I wished for you.
I remember that Christmas
where I sat alone after
spending time with my family.
My apartment was dark
except for the Christmas lights
that shone in the dark like
a thousand little stars.
My body was still healing,
still unknown to me,
I had yet to find my light again.
Though I should have been overjoyed
after receiving so many gifts,
I lamented what I didn't have.
Turning inward, I tried to feel
my way along every crevice,
every hill and valley inside of me.
I tried to come to terms with
what my life was like now,
my body that held me so tightly
that I often found myself short of breath.
I ran a finger along my skin,
trying to see if I could feel
that which no one could see.

I looked into the lights,

shining like so many stars,

and imagined them as candles

burning brightly in the night sky.

I let out a deep breath and said:

"I wish for someone to love me as I am. I wish for someone to love me completely."

I closed my eyes and imagined

that I could feel the stars

gently caressing my eyelids.

With my eyes closed,

the room seemed to grow brighter

as if giving me an answer to my wish.

Months later, when we met,

I remember the light that shone

above your head, as if you had a halo.

I was reminded of those Christmas lights,

shining like multi-coloured stars.

It was as if the light was telling me

that it was granting my wish,

as if it were giving me the gift of you.

Every time you ask me what I want

as a gift, I am befuddled.

I already have everything that I could need,

because I have you.

You truly are the greatest gift,

for you love all of me beyond all imagination.

My only hope is that you know

how much I value you,

how much I love you
and how thankful I am
that my wish was granted.

You Are...

* This poem is for my Writing Sister Kimberlee

You are my Sister,
there is a bond between us
that goes deeper than blood.
You are a Warrior,
never buckling under pressure,
you fight the battle of your life.
You are an Angel,
one of those rare people
that live beyond their bodies.
You are a Light,
filling the world around you
with stars and the sun.
You are Kindness,
making the world a better place,
just by being in it.
You are Magic,
able to create visions out of
ink and paint so real they live.
You are Love
and everything that it stands for,
you redefine what love is.
You are part of me,
and you are part of my dreams.
I only hope that they inspire you
to live yours.

Living Beyond the Waves

I am within the waves.
They are filling my world with noise,
with a torrent of force that
sweeps me through life,
deciding my direction
and taking away my choice.
I go where they take me,
where the waters bring me.
I try to keep my head above water,
attempt to quiet the battle
happening within me and outside of me,
but the force of the water
and the war inside of me is too great.
I dig down deep inside myself
and find a seed of courage.
As I hold it, its warmth spreads through me,
and the noise of the waves softens.
It is as if I am inside of myself and
all I can hear is the hum of that seed,
all I can feel is its heat sliding up my arm.
I look through the waves and see land,
a terrain that I find unfamiliar and foreign.
I know that, even though it is unknown to me,
that it is my salvation. With all my might,
I swim towards that piece of land,
that sliver of green that I can see
through the deep blue of the waves.

The waves sense my growing courage
and they amplify their force,
strengthen their torrent until I am
all but lost under the waters.
Through the sliver of waves that I can see,
a hand appears and grasps mine.
I grab hold of it and let whoever
the hand belongs to pull me to safety.
I let the hand pull me further towards
the piece of land that I was able to glimpse
and it is as green as I had hoped,
full of vegetation and light.
I look to the person who saved me
and am astounded to be looking at myself.
I regard myself for a moment.
He is the me that I used to be.
He is pale from weakness and lack of sun,
but he offers me a smile.
"You looked like you could use some help"
He said.
I nodded and said **"Thank you."**
"Thank yourself. You helped me, now it is my turn to help you."
"I don't understand." I tell him.
My past self gives me a sage look.
*"You don't have to live amongst the waves. You can choose the
direction of your life."*
I look back at the waves.
"Sometimes, I feel as if I'm drowning."

"Then make another choice. Choose to live instead of merely surviving."

I nod as if I comprehend. But then I say:

"I do pretty well but sometimes, I forget to do that."

He takes my hand holding the seed of courage
and unfurls my fingers.

"When you forget how, use this. It's what it's for. Here…"

He takes the seed and presses it into
palm of my hand. The heat increases
until my body is alight with the warmth and light
that I felt from the seed. I can feel it
swimming within me.

"Live beyond the waves."

He whispers.

I turn to look at the waves
at the tumultuous embrace they promise.
When I turn back, he is gone from my sight
but I can feel him within me.
I turn my back on the sound of water
and instead turn to take in the land
that spreads before me. I take one step
and then another. I look up to the sky and
feel the warmth of the sunshine
echoed in that small seed of courage.

"I will live beyond the waves."

I say and take another step
towards my future.

About the Author

Jamieson is an award-winning author of over forty books including the Number One Best Seller, Talking to the Sky, Walking on the Earth and Dancing with the Flame.

He is also an accomplished artist. He works in mixed media, charcoal, pastels and oil paints.

He currently lives in Ottawa, Ontario, Canada with his cat, Tula, who is fearless.

Learn more about Jamieson at www.JamiesonWolf.com

www.ingramcontent.com/pod-product-compliance
Lightning Source LLC
Chambersburg PA
CBHW071528040426
42452CB00008B/929